AMERICAN WAR BIOGRAPHIES

Benedict Arnold

Karen Price Hossell

Heinemann Library
Chicago, Illinois

©2004 Heinemann Library
a division of Reed Elsevier Inc.
Chicago, Illinois

Customer Service 888-454-2279
Visit our website at www.heinemannlibrary.com

Designed by Heinemann Library
Page layout by Lisa Buckley
Maps by John Fleck and Heinemann Library
Photo research by Janet Lankford Moran
Printed and bound in China by South China Printing
  Company Limited

08 07 06 05 04
10 9 8 7 6 5 4 3 2 1

Library of Congress Cataloging-in-Publication Data
Price Hossell, Karen, 1957-
  Benedict Arnold / Karen Price Hossell.
      p. cm. -- (American war biographies)
  Summary: Profiles Benedict Arnold, an accomplished soldier of
the French and Indian War and the Revolutionary War who is best
remembered as a traitor and spy for the British during his time as
commander of West Point.
  Includes bibliographical references (p.) and index.
  ISBN 1-4034-5078-1 (library binding : hardcover) -- ISBN
1-4034-5085-4 (paperback)
  1. Arnold, Benedict, 1741-1801--Juvenile literature. 2.
American loyalists--Biography--Juvenile literature. 3. Generals--
United States--Biography--Juvenile literature. 4. United States.
Continental Army--Biography--Juvenile literature. [1. Arnold,
Benedict, 1741-1801. 2. American loyalists. 3. Generals. 4. United
States--History--Revolution, 1775-1783.] I. Title. II. Series.
  E278.A7P75 2004
  973.3'82'092--dc22

                                    2003021783

Acknowledgments
The author and publisher are grateful to the following for
permission to reproduce copyright material:
pp. 4, 7 National Archives and Records Administration; pp. 9, 11,
14, 19, 30, 31 Bettmann/Corbis; p. 17 Lee Snider/Corbis; p. 25
New York Historical Society, New York, USA/Bridgeman Art
Library; pp. 27, 33, 37, 43 Library of Congress; pp. 35, 41, 42
North Wind Picture Archives; p. 39 The Granger Collection, New
York

Cover photograph by Hulton Archive/Getty Images

Special thanks to Gary Barr for his help in the preparation
of this book.

Some words are shown in bold, **like
this.** You can find out what they mean
by looking in the glossary.

Contents

Chapter One: Benedict Arnold and the Revolutionary War 4

Chapter Two: Young Benedict Arnold 6

Chapter Three: Arnold Becomes a Soldier 8

Chapter Four: Arnold Becomes a Businessman 10

Chapter Five: Attack on Fort Ticonderoga 12

Chapter Six: Attacking Quebec 18

Chapter Seven: Fighting the British on Lake Champlain 24

Chapter Eight: Arnold's Troubles 26

Chapter Nine: Humiliation and Bravery 28

Chapter Ten: Military Governor of Pennsylvania 32

Chapter Eleven: Traitor 36

Chapter Twelve: The Story Ends 40

Chapter Thirteen: Benedict Arnold's Legacy 42

Timeline 44

Further Reading 45

Glossary 46

Index 48

The Revolutionary War was fought between American **colonists** and the British. It officially began on April 19, 1775, in Lexington, Massachusetts. By the end of that day, eleven soldiers were dead and many more were wounded.

Patriots and Loyalists

Years before the war began, colonists were dividing into two groups. One group, called **Loyalists,** believed that the colonies should remain a part of Great Britain. The other group was the **Patriots.** Many Patriots

This painting depicts American colonists cheering as tea is dumped into Boston Harbor.

believed that the colonies should be totally free from British rule. Other Patriots felt that the colonies could remain tied to Great Britain, but that they should have more freedom.

Patriots were angry with Britain's lawmaking body, called **Parliament,** because Parliament kept making the colonists pay taxes. Beginning in the 1760s, colonists were forced to pay taxes on tea, sugar, newspapers, and other items. Colonists felt that they should have a say in the laws they were made to follow and the taxes they were made to pay. But colonists had no representation and no vote in Parliament.

The Boston Tea Party

Patriots were also concerned about other things the British were doing. In December 1773 Patriots protested the British tea tax by throwing tea into Boston Harbor. This event was called the Boston Tea Party. To punish the Patriots, Parliament ordered British troops to move into Boston to make sure that nothing like this happened again. Then Parliament closed Boston Harbor, which meant that the British controlled which ships sailed in and out.

Benedict Arnold

By April of 1775, tensions had risen even more. Patriots who had thought that the colonies could be content under British rule were changing their minds and agreeing with those who wanted complete independence from Great Britain.

One such Patriot was Benedict Arnold. Arnold was a general in the Continental army, which was the army of the American colonies. He had a reputation for bravery, and the commander-in-chief of the army, George Washington, respected and trusted Arnold. But before the war was over, Arnold turned away from the Patriot cause. He became a Loyalist and **betrayed** the Patriots. His actions during the Revolution made him the most famous **traitor** in American history.

1741

Benedict Arnold
is born

1753

Arnold becomes
an apprentice

Benedict Arnold was born on January 14, 1741, in Norwich Town, Connecticut. His family had deep roots in the area. In fact, his mother's family was among those who helped found Norwich Town. One of Benedict Arnold's ancestors, also named Benedict Arnold, was elected governor of the colony of Rhode Island ten times. Arnold's father was a wealthy **merchant** who owned ships that sailed to faraway ports and traded goods. His mother belonged to a religious group called the **Puritans,** who believed in a simple form of worship.

Education

Young Benedict went to a one-room school until he was eleven. Then his parents sent him to a boarding school in Canterbury, Connecticut. At this school he studied English, mathematics, the Bible, languages such as Latin, history, and the ancient Greeks and Romans. Benedict was especially good at Latin and math.

When school let out for the summer, Benedict joined his father on sailing expeditions. Usually they sailed to islands in the **Caribbean** called the West Indies, where they traded goods and picked up items to sell in the north.

When his father became very sick, his mother took Benedict out of boarding school. His father had turned to drinking and did not pay as much attention to his business as he should have. When Benedict was thirteen, the business collapsed.

This engraving of Benedict Arnold was published in 1879. It depicts Arnold during the height of his military career.

After that, Benedict remained in Norwich Town. He spent a great deal of time outdoors, ice skating, fishing, and hunting. Benedict made friends with some of the local Mohegan Indians. They showed him how to get along in the woods and the best ways to hunt and trap animals. By this time, Benedict was taller than most other boys his age. He was also a born leader, and the boys in his neighborhood looked up to him.

Apprentice

It was not unusual in those days for boys who were twelve and thirteen to become **apprentices.** At thirteen, Benedict's mother sent him to be an apprentice to her relative, Dr. Daniel Lathrop. Dr. Lathrop also lived in Norwich and was an **apothecary,** or druggist. In his shop Benedict learned how to sell and mix drugs and medicine, and he also learned about how to run a business. Benedict lived with the Lathrops for eight years, and he and the Lathrop family grew close during that time.

The Lathrops were a wealthy family, and Benedict paid close attention to how they handled money. Soon, though, Benedict became interested in something else— being a soldier.

3 Arnold Becomes a Soldier

1754

French and Indian
War begins

1758

Arnold joins
a militia in
New York

1759

Arnold again
joins a militia
in New York

Arnold's mother
dies

1760

Arnold rejoins
militia unit to
fight in the
French and
Indian War

In 1754 a war began in the colonies over ownership of land in the western part of Pennsylvania and the Ohio River Valley. The French convinced some American Indians to help them fight against the English and the American colonists. This was called the **French and Indian War.**

In 1757 Benedict Arnold decided that he wanted to fight in the war, even though he was only sixteen. Because he was an **apprentice** to Dr. Lathrop, Arnold had to get his permission to join the army. Dr. Lathrop allowed him to go to Fort William Henry in New York to fight. With other men from Norwich, Arnold marched to the fort. The men returned a week later, however, because they were not needed to fight.

But Arnold still wanted to be a soldier. In March of 1758, he left the Lathrop house and walked all the way to New York. There, he joined up with a **militia** led by Captain Reuben Lockwood. With the militia, he marched north to help the British fight the French at Fort Ticonderoga.

When Arnold's mother discovered what her son had done, she sent someone to bring him home. Not surprisingly, Arnold was embarrassed by this. He went back to Norwich Town and resumed his apprenticeship with Dr. Lathrop.

But Arnold's desire to be a soldier was so strong that a year later he ran away again to join troops fighting in the war. Dr. Lathrop actually placed an ad in a newspaper promising a reward to the person who brought Arnold back to Norwich Town. It worked, and Arnold was returned home.

Not long after that, however, Arnold heard that many volunteers were needed to fight in the war. This time he went to his mother to talk her into letting him go. Finally, she agreed, and he went to New York to join troops there. During training, Arnold's fellow soldiers were impressed by how well he could shoot and how far he could march without getting tired. He did not stay in New York long. Only a few months after he arrived for training he found out that his mother was very sick. He went back home to be with her. She died on August 15, 1759. On March 26, 1760, Arnold rejoined his militia unit. Later that year, when much of the fighting in the war had died down, Arnold returned home.

The French and Indian War, also called the Seven Years' War, was fought in North America from 1754 to 1763. The war was fought between the French and the British for land and trade rights.

4   Arnold Becomes a Businessman

1762
Arnold opens his
own shop

1763
Arnold buys his
first ship

1765
Parliament passes
the Stamp Act

1767
Arnold marries
Margaret
Mansfield

1774
Arnold is a
delegate to the
Continental
Congress

1775
Arnold leads New
Haven militia

Back in Norwich Town, Arnold went back to work for Dr. Lathrop. Instead of working as an **apothecary,** however, Arnold went to work on one of the ships Lathrop owned. The doctor used the ships to trade in much the same way Arnold's father had. Arnold went on voyages to the **Caribbean** and to London. He learned about how to make money in international trade.

Then Arnold decided to open up his own apothecary shop. Dr. Lathrop gave him the money to buy the shop and supplies, and Arnold moved to New Haven, Connecticut, to open up his shop. The shop was much like a general store. Arnold sold jewelry, accessories, books, stationery, and cosmetics. Many of the items he sold were imported from London.

Arnold continued to find ways to make money. In 1763 he bought a large **sloop** called *Fortune.* He sailed the ship from Canada to the Caribbean, using his knowledge of trading as he bought and sold goods in different countries. His business did so well that he was able to buy three more ships by 1766.

The Stamp Act

In 1765 the English **Parliament** imposed a Stamp Act on the American colonies. This meant that Americans had to pay a tax to have a stamp put on many goods, such as newspapers and other paper items. Like many Americans, Arnold protested against the Stamp Act and other taxes that Parliament forced colonists to pay. He joined a group called the Sons of Liberty. Arnold and the other members of the group decided that they would do anything to stop the Stamp Act—even commit acts of violence. Soon, Arnold became well known in New Haven and was a respected political leader.

Smuggling

Although he was a businessman and political leader, Benedict Arnold made much of his money illegally. Like many Americans during his time, Arnold was a **smuggler.** This means that he imported and exported goods without paying taxes on them. Many **Patriots** looked the other way when they heard about smuggling. They figured the tax money and **customs** that honest merchants paid went directly to the British anyway, and they were tired of the British taxes. Arnold helped his smuggling business when on February 22, 1767, he married Margaret Mansfield. Her father was a sheriff, so he protected Arnold from being caught.

Rumors of war

In August of 1774, Arnold was named as a **delegate** from Connecticut to the first meeting of the American Congress, called the First **Continental Congress.** In March of 1775, he became the captain of a New Haven **militia** company. All through the colonies, rumors spread that a war would soon be starting with Great Britain. In April 1775 the rumors became true.

These are a few examples of the stamps needed for various goods under the Stamp Act of 1765.

Militia

In colonial times, many regions formed militia groups. They were made up of armed men who joined together to defend their cities, towns, and villages. Most men were expected to become members of an area's militia. A few times a year, the militia would meet to practice loading and firing muskets and to drill, or march, on the town green. During the Revolutionary War—especially at the beginning—militia units banded together to defend their areas against the British. As the war continued, however, the Continental army did most of the fighting.

1775

April 18
General Gage
orders British
soldiers to
destroy weapons
depot at Concord

April 19
Battles at
Lexington and
Concord

April 23
American Congress
orders nearly
14,000 soldiers to
prepare for war

May 10
Arnold and Allen
capture Fort
Ticonderoga

May 10
The Second
Continental
Congress opens
in Philadelphia

On April 19, 1775, about seventy **militiamen** from Massachusetts faced British soldiers who were advancing on Lexington Green. The British troops were on their way to the city of Concord, following orders from British General Gage to destroy the weapons **depot** there. Gage had ordered about 700 British troops to Concord. Those marching into Lexington were advance troops, sent ahead to find out what kind of situation the rest of the soldiers would face.

It is not known which side fired first, but a shot rang out. The British fired at the militiamen and then charged them with **bayonets.** When the fighting was over, eight Americans were dead and ten were wounded. The British continued on to Concord. After destroying the weapons depot, they met up with another group of Americans at Concord's North Bridge. Three British soldiers were killed in fighting there.

The fighting at Lexington and Concord marked the start of the Revolutionary War. As the news of the fighting spread, militia groups around the colonies began to march on Boston, where thousands of British soldiers were stationed. Soon, more than 20,000 militiamen were camped outside Boston. They planned to attack the British and force them out of the city. The militia, however, had few supplies. They were low on weapons and ammunition and had little means of getting them.

Arnold's plan

Benedict Arnold came up with a plan to get cannons for the Americans. He knew that there were cannons at Fort

Ticonderoga, a British post in northern New York, and at nearby Fort Amherst at Crown Point. There were only about 40 men defending Fort Ticonderoga because most of the British soldiers in the colonies were now in Boston. Besides being a source for weapons, the location of the fort was an important one because it was between British North America—now called Canada—and New York. If the Americans could capture the fort, they would have an important outpost.

Arnold wrote down a plan that explained how he could attack the forts, capture the cannons and other weapons, and transport them to Boston. The Massachusetts **Committee of Safety,** which was in charge of military planning for that colony, agreed that his idea was a good one. They made Arnold a **colonel** and gave him money and supplies for the trip to Fort Ticonderoga. On May 3, he and his aides started out.

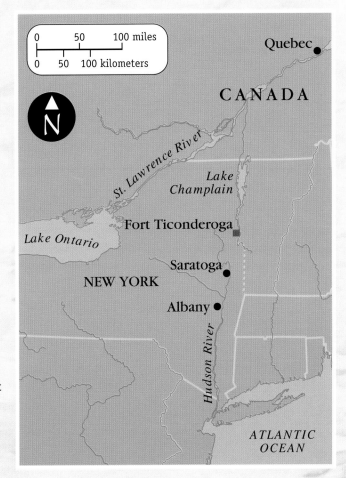

Fort Ticonderoga was valuable because of its location, controlling important waterways into Canada. It was also valuable because of its stores of weapons and ammunition.

Ethan Allen was born on January 21, 1738, in Litchfield, Connecticut. Allen died on February 12, 1789. He was 51 years old.

Ethan Allen

Like Benedict Arnold, Ethan Allen was born in Connecticut. As an adult, he moved to the New Hampshire Grants, which later became Vermont. Allen put together a militia group, called the Green Mountain Boys, to defend against New Yorkers who were trying to take over land in the New Hampshire Grants. After helping to capture Fort Ticonderoga, Allen was captured by the British and held prisoner until 1778. Later, he became involved in Vermont politics.

Ethan Allen and the Green Mountain Boys

Soon, Arnold discovered that another militia group had heard of his idea and was also planning an attack on Fort Ticonderoga. This group was from the New Hampshire Grants—the present state of Vermont—and was called the Green Mountain Boys. They were led by Ethan Allen. Arnold was not happy when he heard about them. He told his men to hurry so they would get to the fort before the Green Mountain Boys.

On the way to Fort Ticonderoga, Arnold met up with Allen at Castleton, Vermont. The two men discussed who should be in charge of the raid. Arnold felt he should lead because he was an officer in the Continental army. But the Green Mountain Boys declared that they would take orders from no one but Allen. The two men finally agreed that they would share command equally, each man leading his own troops.

Attacking the fort

On the evening of May 9, more than 200 of Arnold's and Allen's **militiamen** waited on the shores of Lake Champlain. They were waiting for boats to take them across the lake to the fort. One boat finally arrived, but it would only hold about 40 men. The boat sailed across the lake twice, and 83 men made it across. They then approached the fort in the early morning hours of May 10.

The soldier guarding the fort was asleep, as were most of the soldiers inside it. Because news took a long time to spread in those days, the British soldiers did not know about the fighting at Lexington and Concord. They had no reason to think they would be attacked and were not prepared to defend the fort. The guard tried to fire his gun at the attackers, but it would not work. Another guard rushed toward the Americans. He tried to use his weapon to attack Arnold, but Arnold struck at the guard with his sword and knocked him down. The guard was surprised but unhurt. The Americans rushed into the fort. They already knew its layout because before they attacked they had asked a young boy who sometimes played inside the fort to draw it for them. The boy's name was Nathan Beman.

Looters

Once inside, the Green Mountain Boys ran around, stealing what they could find. Benedict Arnold watched unhappily as they **looted** the fort, and he tried to stop them. But the story goes that Allen wanted his men to be able to keep looting. He pulled out his gun, aimed it at Arnold, and forced Arnold to turn over command to him.

Arnold and his men decided to look for the cannons they had come to get. They discovered more cannons than they expected to, although many of them were in bad shape. Some were half-buried under soil, and others were under water. The Americans made the 42 British soldiers, along with their wives and children, their prisoners of war.

Arnold, Allen, and their militiamen remained at the fort to protect it from British invasion. Several weeks later, Colonel Henry Knox, who was in charge of the Continental army **artillery,** came to get the cannons. Knox and his men moved the cannons across New York and into Massachusetts, where they set them up on hills above Boston.

Arnold and Allen disagree

At Fort Ticonderoga, Arnold and Allen argued over what had happened during the **ambush.** Arnold, who liked organization and order, thought the Green Mountain Boys had acted badly during the ambush. Many of them left soon after they captured the fort, and they took the items they had stolen with them. Allen and other Green Mountain Boys tried to make it look as though they had done most of the work.

Arnold wrote a report about the surprise attack on Fort Ticonderoga and sent it back to military headquarters in Cambridge, Massachusetts, with messengers. But the messengers were Green Mountain Boys. The report, which described the role Arnold and his men played in the raid, never made it to Cambridge. Instead, it mysteriously disappeared.

A naval attack

Soon Arnold had another plan. With some of his men, he sailed a **sloop** named *Liberty* to Quebec, which at that time was a British colony. There, on Lake Champlain, he planned to take over a British ship named *George*, after the British king. When Allen found out that Arnold was doing this, he decided that he and his men would find boats and race the *Liberty* to the *George*. But *Liberty* reached the *George* first, and on May 19, 1775, Arnold and his men attacked. They were so quiet that the British had no time to grab their weapons. The Americans successfully took control of the *George* without firing a single shot. They renamed the *George* the *Enterprise*. After taking the *George*, Arnold's men went to nearby Fort St. Johns and attacked it. There they found four more small boats, which they took.

Arnold's attack on the *George* was the first naval attack in American history. It was also the first time Americans invaded a foreign country.

This modern-day picture shows the south barracks at Fort Ticonderoga, New York. Many old cannons are still positioned around the fort.

As Arnold and his men returned to Fort Ticonderoga, they ran into Ethan Allen and his Green Mountain Boys. The Green Mountain Boys were cold, tired, and hungry, so Arnold's men helped them go back to the fort. Arnold and Allen met and decided that the competition between them had to end. They realized that they would get more done if they worked together.

1775

June 3
Arnold is told
to give up his
command at Fort
Ticonderoga

August 20
George
Washington
makes Arnold a
captain in the
Continental army

September
Arnold and his
men journey
to Quebec

November 3
Arnold's troops
reach Canada

November 13
First attack
on Quebec

December 31
Second attack
on Quebec

For two months, Arnold and his men occupied Fort Ticonderoga and controlled more than 100 miles of **frontier.** At first Congress was happy to hear about the capture of the fort and its weapons. But soon American politicians became concerned. They had not officially authorized such drastic measures, and they thought Arnold had behaved too independently.

Meanwhile, Arnold was again annoyed by Ethan Allen. Allen and the Green Mountain Boys were still in northern New York, and they were making plans to invade British-owned Canada. Arnold had already been planning the same thing and had much of his plan worked out. He explained his plan to Congress, but they decided the attack should wait.

Congress investigates

However, Congress did decide to investigate Benedict Arnold's actions at Fort Ticonderoga. They thought he had made too many decisions without consulting them. Then American leaders sent another **colonel** named Benjamin Hinman to Fort Ticonderoga, along with about 600 **reinforcements.** Hinman told Arnold that he had been ordered to take over for Arnold in the area. But Arnold said he had not been informed of the change and that he would not turn over his command to Hinman until he had official notice to do so.

On June 3, 1775, three Massachusetts politicians came to the fort and told Arnold he had to step down. He could still lead the Massachusetts **militia,** but he had to give his command of the fort, along with much of northern New

This picture shows Quebec around 1775. The city was built on a cliff (visible in the background), which made it a hard target to attack. In the foreground, soldiers land on the coast to prepare for battle.

York, to Hinman. Arnold refused and asked for a hearing. On June 24, he **resigned** as leader of the Massachusetts militia. After resigning, Arnold set off for New Haven. Along the way he found out that his wife had suddenly died and that his sister, Hannah, was taking care of his three sons.

Colonel Arnold

Although Arnold was in trouble with leaders in Massachusetts as well as some in Congress, General George Washington still trusted him. On August 20, Washington made Arnold a colonel in the Continental army. Then Washington ordered Arnold to take his men and attack Quebec, which was a walled city that became British territory in 1759. When attacking, though, Arnold had to do three things. First, he had to treat the Canadians as fellow Americans. Second, he had to prove that he did not act wrongly at Fort Ticonderoga. Third, he had to try to meet up with Major General Philip Schuyler's forces in the north. Schuyler was the head of the northern forces.

When Arnold and his men linked up with Schuyler, said Washington, Arnold had to agree that he would follow Schuyler's orders.

Arnold selects his army

Washington and Arnold went to Continental army camps just outside Boston. There, Washington told Arnold he could select 1,000 men to join him in the attack on Quebec. Many soldiers thought the Canadian mission sounded exciting, and they jumped at the chance of fighting with Arnold, who had a good reputation in the army. Arnold ended up with almost 5,000 volunteers instead of 1,000.

Since he could not use that many men, Arnold decided to take only men who were tall and less than 30 years old. Then he asked each volunteer some questions. First, he asked each man if he was an active woodsman— that is, if he knew how to live and travel in the wilderness and was able to hunt. Then he asked if the men knew how to use **bateaux,** which are small boats. Arnold planned to have 200 bateaux built to carry his army across the St. Lawrence River into Quebec. Because they wanted to go with Arnold, many men lied and said yes. He ended up taking 947 men from the Continental army.

The mission begins

On September 11, 1775, Arnold gathered his men on Cambridge Commons in Massachusetts. The army set out for Quebec the next day, and Arnold and his staff left Cambridge on September 15. In the army were 252 riflemen and woodsmen with scalping knives and tomahawks. The army was to head north to the Kennebec River in Maine. There they would sail farther north to where the bateaux were being readied.

But the journey was more difficult than expected. The area was deep wilderness and hard to navigate. The 200 bateaux turned out to be poorly made because the men who built them were really not experienced at boatbuilding. As they trudged through the wilderness and tried to sail up the shallow river, the soldiers ran out of food. Then the river flooded, and

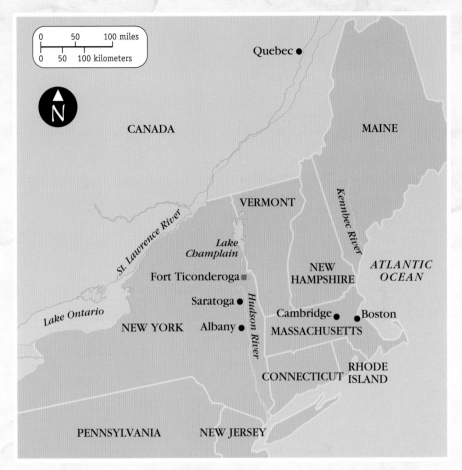

The journey from Cambridge to Quebec was about 400 miles. In the 1700s, traveling through wilderness and by boat, that was a difficult journey taking several days.

they lost some supplies as boats overturned. To add to their problems, it was later discovered that the maps Arnold had been given before he left were no good. They had been drawn by British explorers, and incorrect versions of the maps were published to mislead enemies of the British.

A hard journey

As the journey grew longer, the American troops began to run out of food and supplies. The men grew so hungry that they chewed on candles, hoping to get some nutrition from the wax. At one point some of Arnold's officers held a meeting and decided to turn back. About one-third of Arnold's soldiers joined them.

The rest of the men reached Canada on November 3. It was freezing cold and there was little to eat. Many men became sick. Some got lost and were never seen again. The men ate anything they could find, including a soldier's pet dog, tree roots, and bark. They even boiled their leather shoes and cartridge boxes and made a kind of soup out of them. Finally, some Canadians who knew the American soldiers were on their way brought them some food. They brought cattle, which Arnold's remaining troops killed and ate. By the time they reached Canada, only about 650 men remained in Arnold's regiment. Many had **deserted.** The others had died.

The first attack

One of the first things Arnold did when he arrived in Canada was visit the leaders of small towns surrounding Quebec. He assured the Canadians that the Americans would be able to fight and win against the British, and that Canada would get back the land the British had claimed. Because the weather was so bad, Arnold's army had to sit outside Quebec for five days. The British discovered Arnold's planned attack when they captured a messenger with a letter from Arnold discussing the plan. Arnold sent scouts to examine the **fortified** city. They came back with the news that there were now more than 1,000 British soldiers defending Quebec.

Then a strange thing happened. The British soldiers guarding the city's main gate lost the keys to the gate and had to leave it open all night. Arnold decided to take advantage of the open gates and rush into the city at night. On November 13, the Americans attacked. The residents of Quebec ran out, and Arnold thought they were fleeing. He was wrong. The citizens were just going to get weapons to prepare to defend the city. When Arnold realized what was happening, he and his men retreated. They knew they were unable to fight against so many British soldiers and Canadians.

By December 5, 300 American **reinforcements** had arrived with General Richard Montgomery, who was replacing the ill Schuyler. Montgomery and his troops had captured the Canadian city of Montreal on November 13— the same day Arnold and his men had tried to attack Quebec.

The second attack

The second attack on Quebec was to take place before December 31, because at midnight on that date the **enlistment period** of most of the Americans ran out. This meant that the men would be free to go home. During a snowstorm at midnight on December 31, the attack began. Very quickly a British soldier fired cannons at the Americans, and General Montgomery was killed. When they realized their leader was dead, many of Montgomery's men fled.

Arnold and his men, however, were not aware of Montgomery's death. They waited for him and his **regiment.** Suddenly, Quebec's Governor Carleton and a mob of British soldiers charged out of the city and into Arnold's troops. Arnold was shot in the leg and carried away by some of his men.

The attack was a failure. About 50 Americans were killed, and nearly 300 were taken prisoner. Arnold and his men went to Montreal, which had already been taken by the Americans. He continued to try to lay **siege** to Quebec, but gave up when a large number of reinforcements arrived from England to help defend the city.

In Montreal, Arnold and his army suffered because they did not have enough food, clothing, or other supplies. Two congressmen gave Arnold permission to seize the goods they needed from **Loyalist** merchants in Montreal. But while Arnold tried to keep track of what his men seized, some **militiamen** saw this as an opportunity to **loot** the city. They paid for some goods, but stole others, and did not keep track of which was which. Later, this got Arnold into trouble.

7 Fighting the British on Lake Champlain

1776

September 12
First naval battle
on Lake
Champlain

October 11
Second naval
battle on Lake
Champlain

After they left Montreal, Benedict Arnold and what was left of his army went back to the fort at Crown Point. There, Arnold began to make plans to put together the first American navy. He knew that thousands of British soldiers were planning to attack the American **colonies** by coming down from Canada and into New York. Arnold thought that American ships could stop any British ships carrying soldiers and supplies from Canada into New York.

Arnold supervised the building of the first ships of the American navy. He had trouble finding sailors, though, because most able men were already fighting in the Continental army. But by August he and his men had built ten ships and had enough men to sail them. On August 24, 1776, the ten ships sailed up Lake Champlain toward Canada.

Facing the British

The American navy's first meeting with British ships happened on September 12. The British attacked the Americans, and three Americans died. Soon six more ships were completed, and they sailed up Lake Champlain to join Arnold's navy.

On October 11, the British attacked again. This time 60 Americans died, and all of their ships were badly damaged. Still, Arnold and his men managed to sail the ships away from the British. The British were angry that Arnold and his men had escaped.

Arnold and the new navy fought bravely, but in the end they were defeated. They went back to Crown Point, where

Arnold ordered the fort burned to the ground. Because the British had won, Arnold knew they would soon occupy the fort. He did not want them to get the fort or any of the supplies in it. With the fort smoldering behind them, Arnold and his men went on to Fort Ticonderoga.

While the Americans had lost this battle, with Benedict Arnold's help they had proved to the British that they were determined to fight, even if the odds were against them. Arnold's plan had also made the British lose time in their attempt to invade the colonies.

The October 11, 1776, battle on Lake Champlain ended with a British victory. However, the battle ultimately weakened the British navy, and they lost ground elsewhere.

1777

February:
Arnold passed over
for promotion

Benedict Arnold was good at military planning and at leading his troops. But sometimes Arnold got into trouble because he did not like to listen to those who had authority over him and because he occasionally ignored rules. It could be argued, however, that Arnold was sometimes treated unfairly by Congress and others in positions of authority.

Money troubles

During the takeover of Fort Ticonderoga, Arnold spent a lot of his own money to buy supplies for his men. Arnold was a wealthy man, but he had spent thousands of dollars on supplies. Many officers did this, and then submitted **receipts** for their purchases to military authorities so that they could be paid back.

During the Fort Ticonderoga mission, the Massachusetts **Committee of Safety** was in charge of Arnold and his men. But when Arnold submitted his receipts to the committee, they delayed in paying him back. Instead they told Arnold he had to meet with them to explain why he had spent so much money. The committee members did not completely trust Arnold, and they wondered if he was trying to cheat them by saying he had spent more money than he really had.

Although few people knew it at the time, the chairman of the committee, Dr. Benjamin Church, was a spy for the British. Dr. Church knew what a good leader Arnold was, and it is possible that Church delayed Arnold's repayment to frustrate him and to put off any of his military plans.

Finally, the committee agreed to pay the money to Arnold, although it took a long time for him to get it.

Accusations

Arnold also got into trouble for what happened in Montreal after the **siege** at Quebec. While it was not illegal for troops to seize goods from citizens, the way they went about it was questioned. Arnold's claims for repayment for money he had spent in Montreal were also investigated. He was found innocent, however.

Not promoted

Another incident made Arnold angry in February of 1777. The Continental Congress promoted five men to the rank of **major general,** but Arnold was not one of them. Arnold was upset because he was first in line to get the promotion, but had been ignored. Men below him had been given the new title, while Arnold remained a general. Arnold was told this had happened because there could only be a certain number of major generals from each state, and Connecticut already had as many as it was allowed.

Benjamin Church was a Patriot and a medical doctor. He most likely became a spy for the British in order to pay off his massive debts.

While these investigations were going on, Arnold continued to work as a military commander. The accusations against him, however, made Arnold wonder if his work for the colonies was appreciated. Some historians believe that these events marked the beginning of Arnold's dissatisfaction with the **Patriot** cause.

9 Humiliation and Bravery

1777

April
Arnold gathers troops and fights off the British in Connecticut

May
Arnold promoted to major general

October
Arnold leads his men into battle at Saratoga and is injured

In April of 1777, Arnold learned that British troops were planning to attack the American supply base in Danbury, Connecticut. As soon as he heard the news, Arnold rushed from his home and gathered troops to meet the British. Arnold's force was soon joined by other **militia** companies, and they managed to fight off the British troops. When Congress heard about Arnold's brave actions, they voted in May 1777 to promote him to the rank of **major general.** But Arnold was still angry with Congress for passing him over for a promotion in February. He decided to **resign** from the army in July, outraged over what he considered to be Congress's unfairness to him.

Offer from George Washington

At about the same time Arnold was deciding to resign, General George Washington was praising him. Washington thought Arnold would be a good man to **recruit** and lead a new **regiment** of soldiers for the Northern Army. Congress had already received Arnold's **letter of resignation.** However, after Washington recommended Arnold, Congress refused to accept his resignation. When Arnold discovered how highly Washington thought of him, he agreed to accept the position. Soon Arnold was put in charge of one part of the Northern Army, and Major General Schuyler was in charge of the other.

Preparing for battle

In the summer of 1777, the British recaptured Fort Ticonderoga. As American soldiers retreated and marched southward, Arnold realized that they would likely meet up

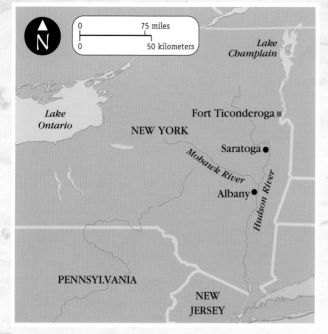

The Battle of Bemis Heights is also known as the Second Battle of Saratoga. British General Burgoyne was running out of supplies and had little choice but to fight through the growing American force at Saratoga in order to make it to Albany.

with British troops. He decided to come up with a plan that would allow the Americans to sneak up on the British and force them to fight. By September 9, Arnold had decided that a spot just upriver from Saratoga, New York, would be the best place to do so. The location was called Bemis Heights.

Arnold's commander was Major General Horatio Gates. He agreed with Arnold's plan and ordered his troops to prepare to fight the British. But on that same day—September 9—Gates and Arnold had a fierce argument. One reason for the argument was Arnold's friendship with Schuyler, whom Gates hated. Several of Schuyler's relatives were on Arnold's staff, and Gates thought Arnold had chosen them just to annoy him. Then Arnold found out that Gates had reversed some of his orders.

Arnold and his men fight

Their arguments were interrupted when the British approached on September 19. The Americans outnumbered the British at Bemis Heights, and Arnold wanted to aggressively attack them. But Gates preferred a more cautious strategy. Arnold led his men into battle, while Gates and his men remained behind. In the end, it was unclear which side won the battle. Arnold again became angry with Gates when he discovered that in the report to Congress about the battle, Gates made no mention of the role Arnold and his men had played. Arnold and Gates had another quarrel,

General Horatio Gates

General Gates was born in England and joined the British army when he was young. He fought in the French and Indian War, then settled in what is now West Virginia in 1772. While George Washington was commander of the Continental army, some people thought Gates should have the job. They worked to remove Washington from his position and replace him with Gates. Historians have not been able to tell whether Gates wanted the job and was involved in the plan to remove Washington. Until 1780, Gates was considered a great military leader. But when he led his troops to a defeat at Camden, South Carolina, in 1780, he was removed from his post. After the war, Gates freed his slaves and moved to New York.

and this time Gates told Arnold that he was taking over his command. This meant that Gates would lead Arnold's troops, who were called the left wing because they fought on the left side of the battlefield. Major General Benjamin Lincoln would take over Gates's men on the right. That left Arnold with nothing to do.

Arnold shows his bravery

Meanwhile, the British were camped nearby. Their leader, General Burgoyne, knew that if he led his men southward, they would most likely meet up with the Americans again and there would be a fierce battle. But on October 7, 1777, General Burgoyne decided that he had no other choice but to lead his troops south toward Albany.

When Benedict Arnold found out that the British were on the move, he went to General Gates with a suggestion of what the Americans should do. But Gates told Arnold to go away, saying, "General Arnold, I have nothing for you to do. You have no business here."

Arnold went back to his tent. He was convinced that his plan was better than anything the cautious Gates would come up with. Finally, he decided to act. He jumped on his horse and raced toward the Connecticut **militia.** When they recognized him, the militiamen cheered. Arnold cried, "Come on brave boys, come on!" The militiamen followed him into battle.

Arnold approached the enemy and charged them. During the battle Arnold was shot in his left leg, the same leg that had been injured in Quebec. Then his horse was shot and killed. The horse fell onto Arnold's injured leg and crushed it.

Arnold was carried off the field. He spent months in the hospital, and more time at home recovering from his wound. He would never again lead men into battle, but he was always remembered for his bravery at Saratoga.

Surrender

Ten days after the Battle of Saratoga, General Burgoyne surrendered to General Gates. Burgoyne and his army of almost 6,000 troops were put on ships and forced to sail back to England. Before they sailed, they were made to promise that they would not come back to fight.

Below, Benedict Arnold is resting on a horse after his injury during the Battle of Saratoga. The British surrender at Saratoga increased the **Patriots'** confidence in the Continental army.

1778

May 30
Arnold becomes
military governor
of Pennsylvania

April 8
Arnold marries
Peggy Shippen

1779

December
Arnold's court-
martial

After Arnold's leg began to heal, he hobbled around on crutches. One day, in May 1778, he showed up at George Washington's headquarters at Valley Forge, Pennsylvania. Arnold said he was ready to return to duty, but Washington told him that his leg would need to heal better before he could return to the army. Instead, Washington suggested that Arnold become the military governor of Pennsylvania.

On May 30, 1778, Arnold accepted the position. At the time, the British were occupying Philadelphia. But the Americans pushed the British out, and they left for good on June 18. The next day, Arnold and his staff moved into the city and took charge. They discovered that the British had destroyed much of Philadelphia. British troops had taken apart many homes to use the wood for firewood. They had knocked over tombstones in cemeteries and broken windows in public buildings.

Quakers

The Quakers are a religious group that started in England in the 1640s. They arrived in the American colonies in 1656. Quakers are also called the Society of Friends. They refuse to carry weapons and to use them against others, so they do not fight in wars. For that reason, many Quakers were wrongly considered to be sympathetic to Great Britain during the Revolutionary War.

In 1779 Benedict Arnold purchased Mount Pleasant and gave it to Peggy Shippen as a wedding present. Because he was charged with treason, the couple never lived there. Mount Pleasant is located in East Fairmount Park, Philadelphia, Pennsylvania.

Mingling with society

Although he and his staff had a lot of work to do to rebuild the city, Arnold seemed to enjoy his time in Philadelphia. While many Philadelphians were **Patriots,** some were **Loyalists.** Several members of Philadelphia society were loyal to the British king, but Arnold mingled with both kinds of people. In November 1778 two **Quakers** that the council of Pennsylvania had declared to be Loyalists were hung. The night before their execution, Arnold showed what many thought to be an expression of sympathy for the Loyalists. He held a party at City Tavern and invited Quakers and Loyalists.

Arnold also began spending a lot of time with the Shippen family, who were wealthy members of Philadelphia society. He was particularly interested in Peggy Shippen. In fact, he fell in love with her. On April 8, 1779, when Peggy was eighteen years old, she and Arnold were married. At the time, Benedict Arnold was 37 years old.

Arnold is criticized

Many city leaders began to criticize Arnold because they believed that he was becoming too close to the Loyalists. Some members of the Shippen family, including Peggy, were known to be **Loyalists,** as were others he associated with. The president of Pennsylvania, Joseph Reed, did not like Arnold. He began accusing Arnold of many things, including spending too much money, being friends with too many Loyalists, and using state-owned wagons to transport his personal goods. Then Congress started investigating some of the accusations. Soon Arnold was facing criminal charges in Pennsylvania. He was cleared of all of the charges except misusing **militia** and wagons to move cargo. Because that was a military matter, Arnold had to face a **court-martial** that would try him on those charges.

Court-martial

The court-martial was held in December of 1779. Arnold was found guilty of two of the charges against him—illegally using a government pass and using government wagons to transport goods. His only punishment was a **reprimand** from George Washington.

But by that time, Arnold was already working as a spy for the British. In April of 1779, he found out that his expenses were being investigated by Congress. He already knew that his finances were in trouble. He had not been paid for his years of work in the military, and because of the war, his business had suffered. He had to borrow thousands of dollars to pay his bills, and he grew more and more frustrated with Congress for not paying him. In May of 1779, needing money and probably encouraged by his wife, Arnold decided to offer his services as a spy to the British.

Peggy Shippen

Peggy Shippen, whose real name was Margaret, was born in 1760. Her father was a well-respected Philadelphia judge. Her family was wealthy and had been involved in Pennsylvania politics for years. Peggy was bright and loved to read, but young women rarely were allowed to attend school past about the eighth grade in those days. Much of what she learned came from reading and having discussions with her father and visitors who came to their home. She was considered one of the city's beauties and attended many parties and balls. She was also friends with John Andre, who in 1780 **recruited** Benedict Arnold as a spy.

11 Traitor

1780

August 2
Arnold becomes
commander of
West Point

September 23
John Andre is
captured and
Arnold escapes

October 2
Andre is hanged

As a spy for the British, Benedict Arnold became involved in a chain of people who passed letters containing information. Arnold was one link in the chain, which was headed by the **Loyalist** William Franklin, the son of **Patriot** Benjamin Franklin. Arnold was given the code names "Monk" and "Mr. Moore."

Codes and invisible ink

The spy network used invisible ink and secret codes to write letters. Usually they would write the code between the lines of a regular letter. The ink was made from water and a chemical called ferrous sulfate. It would show up when placed over heat or when treated with a chemical called sodium carbonate. The secret code Arnold and his spy ring used was a book code. This means that each word in the code was based on a page from a particular book, then a line and word from that page. The person receiving the coded message had to know which book to use to be able to decode the message.

The spy network

Arnold worked with several spies. He worked most closely with a British soldier named John Andre, who was in charge of British Secret Intelligence. Andre wanted Arnold to continue to work for the American side so he could gain information. Andre told Arnold the British would pay him a lot of money for information such as where troops were planning to go and when they would get there. Between Arnold and Andre was a **mediator** named Joseph Stansbury.

Arnold's wife, Peggy, also knew about the letters. As far as historians can tell, no one in the Continental army suspected Arnold of spying.

West Point

On June 29, 1780, George Washington gave Benedict Arnold command of West Point, on the Hudson River in New York. Today West Point is a military academy, but in Arnold's time it was a fort. The fort prevented enemy ships from sailing up the Hudson River. There was even a 500-yard-long chain that floated on logs across the river to keep ships from passing.

After Washington told Arnold he could be commander at West Point, he returned and told Arnold about an even better job. Washington was sure that Arnold would accept the new job, which involved leading the entire left wing of the army. However, Arnold had already told the British that once he was at West Point he would be willing to surrender the fort to them for

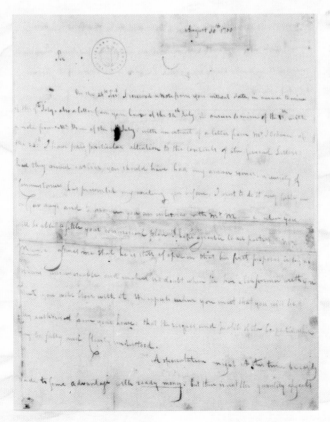

This letter was sent to "John Anderson" (John Andre) from Benedict Arnold. Arnold signed his name "Gustavus" in order to keep his true identity a secret.

20,000 pounds. This is equal to almost 3 million dollars in today's American money. Arnold told Washington that his leg bothered him too much to be on the battlefield, and that he would prefer to go to West Point. Arnold was officially named the fort's commander on August 2.

Arnold worked out a plot with the British to surrender West Point in September of 1780. To make sure that the fort would be easy for the British to capture, Arnold began to weaken the fort's defenses almost as soon as he took charge. He sent some soldiers to do odd jobs and told others he did not need them. When supplies were used up, he did not order new ones, or he ordered too few. All that was needed to complete the plan was for Andre and Arnold to work out the final details.

Discovered

But the surrender of West Point never occurred. On September 23, 1780, American **militiamen** captured John Andre while he was carrying papers from Arnold. Among the papers was information from Arnold about where American troops would be when the British attacked. When Arnold found out about Andre's capture, he fled West Point and went to a British ship, the *Vulture,* which was in the Hudson River. Just before Arnold fled, George Washington arrived at Arnold's home in West Point. Arnold knew Washington was coming. Many of Washington's men believed that Arnold had arranged for Washington to be captured when the British attacked.

Andre was given a **court-martial** and was found guilty. Even though they did not like what he did, many American soldiers admired Andre for his bravery. Some even asked George Washington to spare Andre's life. But Washington felt that he had to be firm and use Andre as an example to other spies. On October 2, 1780, John Andre was hanged.

The events surrounding Andre's execution and Arnold's escape angered many Americans. They believed that the wrong man had died. They saw Arnold as the worst kind of **traitor,** and many wished that Arnold had been hanged instead of Andre. In Arnold's hometown of Norwich Town, Connecticut, townspeople destroyed the tombstones of Arnold's father and brother because they were also both named Benedict Arnold. In Philadelphia, an **effigy** of Arnold was made and paraded through the streets. The effigy had two faces to show that Arnold was two-faced—that is, that he worked for both sides in the war.

John Andre

John Andre spoke several languages. He was a promising artist, as well as a poet and a musician. Andre loved to paint, and he also liked the theater. He wrote plays and acted. When the British occupied Philadelphia during the Revolutionary War, Andre broke into and lived in Benjamin Franklin's house. He read many of Franklin's books and enjoyed looking around Franklin's workshop. He was 31 years old when he was hanged for spying.

In this 19th-century engraving, Benedict Arnold is trying to convince Major John Andre to conceal the plans for the surrender of West Point in his boot at their meeting on September 21, 1780.

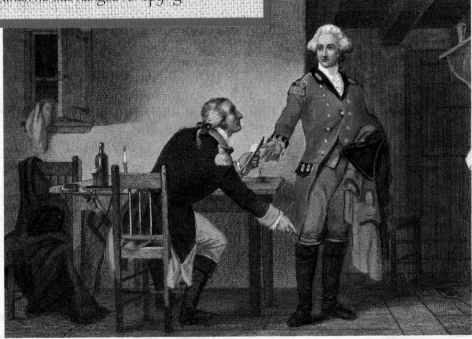

12 The Story Ends

1780
December 11
Arnold's kidnapping is foiled

1781
September
Arnold and the American Legion attack New London, Connecticut

1782
January
The Arnolds sail to England

1785
Arnold goes to Canada to become a lumber businessman

1792
Arnold returns to England

1801
June 14
Arnold dies

1804
Peggy dies

After his **betrayal** of the American cause became known, the British made Benedict Arnold **brigadier general** of **provincial** troops. They also paid Arnold more than 6,000 pounds—about 200,000 dollars in today's American money—for his work as a spy. Arnold then began to **recruit** soldiers for a new British **regiment** called the American Legion. Most of his recruits were **deserters** from the Continental army.

George Washington allowed Peggy Arnold to go to her father's home in Philadelphia. Few people would speak to her, and most turned away from her when they saw her on the street. She was **banished** from the city on October 27, 1780, and went to New York City. Arnold's sons from his first marriage were made members of the British army, even though they were all under age fourteen.

Attempted kidnapping

Some advisors to George Washington came up with a plan to have Arnold **assassinated,** and Washington agreed to the plan. One of Washington's generals, whose name was Light Horse Harry Lee, put Sergeant Major John Champe in charge of the mission. He instructed Champe to act as if he were **defecting** to the British side and to volunteer for Arnold's American Legion. Champe did so and was made a high-ranking official in the Legion. Champe came up with a plan to kidnap Arnold on December 11 while Arnold was on his daily midnight walk in his garden in New York City. Then Arnold would be brought to George Washington, who would have him publicly hanged for **treason.**

But Champe and his helpers never had a chance to kidnap Arnold. On December 11, 1780, the very day of the planned kidnapping, Arnold ordered all of his troops to board ships for a mission to the James River in Virginia. Champe had no choice but to follow orders, and Arnold himself also boarded ship.

Attacking American cities

In Virginia, the American Legion attacked the city of Richmond and burned much of it. Virginia's governor, Thomas Jefferson, quickly announced a large reward for the capture of Benedict Arnold. But Arnold was not caught.

In September 1781, Arnold and his men attacked New London, Connecticut. They destroyed many American ships docked there and burned more than 100 buildings, including homes.

Benedict Arnold is shown here escaping on horseback after his treason was discovered in 1780.

But while Arnold was leading troops against the Americans, he was not very popular with many of the British soldiers. They saw him as a coward who had escaped while John Andre, whom they admired, had been punished. Members of the British army were also jealous of Arnold because he had been given a high command that they felt he did not deserve.

In England and Canada

Near the end of the war, in January 1782, the Arnold family finally sailed to England. They were not well liked by many there, and had a difficult time fitting in. In 1785 Benedict Arnold sailed to Canada, where he stayed for seven years, working in the lumber business. He returned to England in 1792. There, he became very concerned about his reputation, and he often argued with those who called him a **traitor.** He again bought ships and traded in the **Caribbean,** as he had done when he was a young man. With his wife, Peggy, he had seven children. On June 14, 1801, Arnold died at the age of 60. In the summer of 1804, Peggy died at the age of 44.

13 Benedict Arnold's Legacy

It seems like Benedict Arnold was really two people. The first Benedict Arnold was a proud **Patriot** who worked hard and sacrificed much to serve his country. He knew how to win loyalty from his troops, and he bravely led them into battle. He was respected by many, including his commander-in-chief, George Washington.

The second Benedict Arnold was a **traitor.** He became so bitter over what he thought was unfair treatment by Congress and by military leaders that he decided to give up the Patriot cause of independence. He provided secret information to the British and offered to surrender an American fortress to them for money. After his **treason** was discovered, Arnold fled so he would not be punished. Then he led troops against American cities, destroying homes and businesses.

Americans burned Benedict Arnold in **effigy** after his treason was discovered.

While many today remember Arnold for his acts as a traitor, they rarely remember his earlier acts of bravery in service to the Patriots. Today, when people hear the name "Benedict Arnold," they think of one thing—that he was a traitor. In fact, people who are accused of betraying their country, their friends, or their families are often called "Benedict Arnolds." While Benedict Arnold did many good things for the cause of American independence, in the end he was a traitor. Perhaps Arnold is an example of how bitterness can change someone, and how a person can be both good and bad.

Only one month before this proclamation was issued by Arnold, George Washington discovered that he was a traitor. In the proclamation, Arnold tries to persuade American troops to come over to the British side.

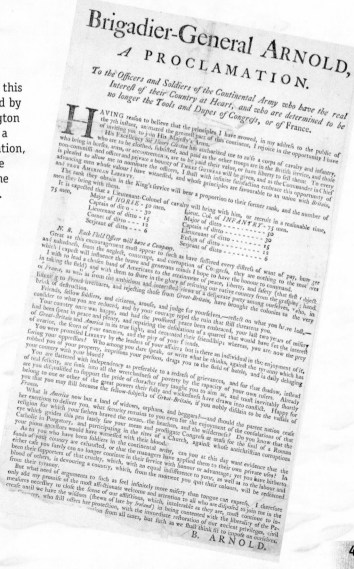

Timeline

April 19, 1775	Battles at Lexington and Concord
April 23, 1775	Massachusetts Congress orders thousands of soldiers to Boston
	Arnold and Allen capture Fort Ticonderoga; the Second **Continental Congress** opens in Philadelphia
July 3, 1775	George Washington takes over leadership of the Continental army
December 23, 1775	England's King George announces that all American colonies are closed to trade
March 1776	Cannons taken from Fort Ticonderoga are placed on Dorchester Heights above Boston
June 28, 1776	In Charleston, South Carolina, American troops fight off the British
June and July 1776	Thousands of British soldiers, ships, and weapons arrive in New York
July 2, 1776	Congress votes to declare independence from Great Britain
July 4, 1776	Congress adopts the Declaration of Independence
August 1776	Battle of Long Island; Washington's troops are defeated; later, the Americans escape northward
October 11, 1776	Led by Benedict Arnold, the American navy has its first conflict and defeat
December 6, 1776	The British capture the naval base at Newport, Rhode Island
December 24–25, 1776	Washington and his troops cross the Delaware River to New Jersey and launch a surprise attack on German forces fighting for the British there; the Germans surrender
April 27, 1777	Benedict Arnold leads troops to victory at Ridgefield, Connecticut
July 6, 1777	British General Burgoyne captures Fort Ticonderoga
September 26, 1777	British forces occupy Philadelphia
October 7, 1777	Battle of Saratoga, led by Generals Gates and Arnold
October 17, 1777	General Burgoyne surrenders to General Gates
November 15, 1777	Congress adopts the Articles of Confederation as the nation's new government
February 1778	The French agree to help the United States win the war
July 10, 1778	France declares war against Great Britain
December 29, 1778	The British capture Savannah, Georgia
September–October 1779	Eight hundred Americans are killed in Savannah
December 26, 1779	The British attack Charleston, South Carolina
May 12, 1780	The British capture Charleston
July 11, 1780	Six thousand French soldiers arrive at Newport, Rhode Island
August 2, 1780	Benedict Arnold is appointed commander at West Point

August 16, 1780	At Camden, South Carolina, American forces are defeated and about 900 Americans are killed
September 23, 1780	John Andre is captured; Benedict Arnold escapes
August 1, 1781	British General Cornwallis and 10,000 British soldiers arrive in Yorktown, Virginia, to rest
August 30, 1781	A French fleet arrives off Yorktown
September 6, 1781	Arnold's troops attack New London, Connecticut
September 28, 1781	Washington and American troops begin the **siege** at Yorktown
October 19, 1781	General Cornwallis officially surrenders at Yorktown
November 10, 1782	The last battle of the war is fought in Ohio territory
February 4, 1783	England announces the war is over

Further Reading

Anderson, Dale. *The American Revolution*. Chicago: Raintree, 2003.

Hossell, Karen Price. *The Boston Tea Party: Rebellion in the Colonies*. Chicago: Heinemann Library, 2003.

Isaacs, Sally Senzell. *America in the Time of George Washington (1747–1803)*. Chicago: Heinemann Library, 1999.

Smolinski, Diane. *Important People of the Revolutionary War*. Chicago: Heinemann Library, 2001.

Smolinski, Diane. *Land Battles of the Revolutionary War*. Chicago: Heinemann Library, 2001.

Smolinski, Diane. *Naval Battles of the Revolutionary War*. Chicago: Heinemann Library, 2001.

Weber, Michael. *The American Revolution*. Chicago: Raintree, 2000.

Glossary

ambush surprise attack

apothecary person who sells drugs and medicine, or a store where those are sold

apprentice someone who promises to work for a set amount of time for someone else while learning a skill or trade

artillery large weapons such as cannons

assassinate murder an important person by a surprise or secret attack

banish force to leave a country, state, city, or other area

bateaux small boats, usually with flat bottoms

bayonet steel blade that attaches to the end of a rifle or a musket, which was a gun used in the Revolutionary War that is similar to a rifle

betray give over to an enemy by treason or fraud; be unfaithful to

brigadier general military officer who is one rank above a colonel

Caribbean sea that is north of South America, east of Central America, and south of the West Indies

colonel army rank above lieutenant colonel and below brigadier general

colonist person who lives in a colony

colony settlement in a new territory that is tied to an established nation

committee of safety group of colonists formed to watch over the safety of the colony. Before the Revolutionary War, committees of safety met to discuss the presence of British troops in their colonies.

Continental Congress group of representatives from the colonies who carried out the duties of the government

court-martial military trial

customs process by which goods are reported and may be taxed upon being brought into a country

defect go over to another side, or escape from one army to the enemy's army

delegate person sent as a representative to a meeting or conference

depot place where things such as military supplies are stored

desert escape military duty without permission

effigy figure made to represent someone

enlistment period amount of time promised to serve, such as in the army or other military branch

fortified strengthened, such as with thick walls or other protections